BRENTON VERSUS

AN EPIC SAGA OF LUST, GRE

S T A R R I N G
(IN ORDER OF APPEARANCE)

DEKE BRENTON

Billionaire head of Chicago's biggest ad agency. The archetypal ruthless business tycoon.

BRETT HOWARD

Deke's only surviving member of staff. A nervous, bespectacled character, rather in the Clark Kent mould. Occasional words in Brett's dialogue are written in a curious phonetic way, spoofing the American habit of mutilating a perfectly good English word by stressing the wrong syllable. The stress falls on the italicised syllable.

FOXGLOVE BRENTON (FOXY)

Deke's daughter. A childish, pathetic creature, with a sing-song voice and heavily affected limp.

LANA BRENTON

Deke's estranged English wife. Glamorous, but deadly.

MATT KIRBY

The family lawyer, and Lana's brother. Sombre, laconic and dead-pan.

BLANCHE DE-VILLE

Deke's first wife. Older than Lana, but otherwise looking how you'd expect someone called Blanche De-Ville to look.

---◆---

*W*hat is the dark secret which enflames the Brenton family feud? Who is the mysterious Eddie? Why are Lana's shoulderpads wider than the door? And just what was Deke Brenton doing down on the farm?

All this, and more, is revealed in this outrageous spoof of American soaps and blockbuster mini-series, set in the manic world of Chicago's biggest advertising agency.

A Flying Ducks Publication

For more information on Flying Ducks Publications, write to *Flying Ducks Publications, Station Road, Highley, Shropshire* WV16 6NW.

ISBN 0 9517267 8 1

BRENTON VERSUS BRENTON

*The setting is a well-appointed office. A venetian blind covers an outside window, behind an impressive desk. On one wall is a sign saying **Brenton & Brenton**. Deke Brenton, multi-billionaire head of Chicago's biggest advertising agency, paces the room, practising a speech, addressing the audience directly. He refers occasionally to a flip chart, with graphs, diagrams, and other visual aids.*

Deke Condoms.

Every year, America spends forty-one billion dollars on condoms. That's more than the United Kingdom's defence budget. And it offers a damn sight more protection. In a typical week, the average American male spends more on condoms than he does on toothpaste. It's a big market, gentlemen.

But you posed us a question. Where's the sales growth coming from next year? Well our research has given us the answer, loud and clear.

Now as you know, in the higher economic groups, Friends condoms are already clearly established as the number one brand, but we're about to help you grab an even bigger share of that lucrative market.

Gentlemen, after months of painstaking research, I give you...the designer condom. For the man who must be smartly dressed, even when he has no clothes on. A condom to aspire to.

This is no simple piece of rubber. This is an extension of the male personality.

Let's take a look around the pack first. Notice that nowhere do we use the word *contraceptive*. Instead, we introduce a new concept - *Lubricated Leisurewear*.

So. Let's take a look in detail at the first ever range of upwardly-mobile condoms.

We have the sports condom, with go-faster stripe. Thermal-lined condoms for the apres ski. The ad-agency condom, complete with designer stubble. And the ultimate gift for the busy Yuppie about town - Filofux - one for every day of the week, neatly bound in a handsome leather wallet.

A Flying Ducks Publication

Forty-one billion dollars, gentlemen. That's a lot of bajookers. Clearly we have the product. And today, I'm going to present to you the advertising campaign that's going to give Friends condoms an even bigger slice of the action than ever before.

We began with a simple proposition. What, at the end of the day, does the average American male actually do in his condom? In a word....(*There's a knock on the door*)...come.

Enter Brett Howard.

Brett You wanted to see me, Mr Brenton?
Deke Brett! Come on in. I've just been running through the presentation for Friends Condom Corporation. Sit yourself down. Coffee?
Brett Thank you.

Deke goes to a coffee percolator at the corner of the room, and fills a plastic cup.

Deke Brett, I've never been one to mince my words.
Brett No, Mr Brenton.
Deke If a poodle craps on my carpet, I say a poodle has crapped on my carpet. I don't say little Fluffy-Wuffs has done a dinky - you know what I mean?
Brett I think so, Mr Brenton.
Deke And then I strangle little Fluffy-Wuffs. Brett, I've been looking through your latest creative ideas for the Friends account, and frankly I don't think it's your best work.
Brett I'm sorry to hear that, Mr Brenton.
Deke You get a chance to work on an account like this once in a lifetime, Brett, and when you do, you've got to grab it. (*He squashes the plastic cup, the contents dribbling all over Brett's crutch. Then he hands the crumpled remains to Brett*) Sugar?
Brett No, thank you.
Deke Friends is an important account to this company, Brett.
Brett It's the only account, Mr Brenton.
Deke No-one's done more than Brenton & Brenton to make Friends condoms the number one brand in the States. Did you know, since we started working on this account, sales have tripled?
Brett Is that so?
Deke That's so, Brett. And it's all down to you. Let's face it, some of your early

work on the Friends account was sheer genius.

Brett Aw, shucks, Mr Brenton...

Deke No I mean it. I mean it. I started thinking to myself, if this boy carries on the way he's going, I'm going to have to change my sign to Brenton, Brenton...and Howard!

Brett Thank you, Mr Brenton.

Deke Oh, don't thank me, Brett. Because I'm about to chew your balls off. What's all this garbage? (*He waves a document in front of Brett's face, and begins quoting from it*) "Next time you screw around, make sure you've got a Friend with you."

Brett Well, it's a way of name branding with...

Deke Name branding my ass! And this TV commercial. You seriously expect me to use this rock and roll song?

Brett Rock and roll's becoming very popular with the kids again, Mr Brenton.

Deke Yeah, but "Johnney B. Goode"? Goddammit Brett, what are you trying to do to me, uh? I'm trying to present a quality image here. We're asking people to pay twenty-five dollars for this pack. Where are the selling points?

Brett I've been working on an idea to attack the price objection, Mr Brenton. (*He hands Deke a piece of paper*)

Deke "Friends condoms. At twenty-five dollars a pack, you get screwed twice". You're not taking this seriously, are you, Brett?

Brett I'm sorry you don't like the ideas, Mr Brenton.

Deke Look, Brett, let's talk. (*Brett tries to say something*) Shut up! Me first. (*Forced smile*) Brett. How are things at home? How's that cute sister of yours, er...

Brett Henrietta.

Deke Did he? I'm sorry to hear that. But apart from that, how are you all settling in? How's the family like Chicago?

Deke peeks through the blind, and we hear a wailing police siren.

Brett They're getting used it.

Deke It's a tough city, Brett. And you don't get to the top by staying at the bottom - you know what I mean?

Brett No, sir.

Deke Brett, when I came to Chicago twenty years ago, I hadn't got a nickel in my pocket. And now, I've got a nickel in my pocket.

Brett That's impressive, Mr Brenton.

Deke You're not from around these parts, are you?

Brett No, sir.

Deke Let me guess - New Jersey?

Brett No, it's just something I feel comfortable in.

Deke No, I mean where are you from?

Brett Oh, Baltimore.

Deke Look, Brett, how long have we been friends now?

Brett About two and a half minutes, Mr Brenton.

Deke Good God, is it as long as that? You know, you're an important member of the team here at Brenton and Brenton.

Brett I'm the only member of the team, Mr Brenton.

Deke Brett, if anything's bugging you, I need to know.

Brett Well, as a matter of fact, Mr Brenton, there is something I...

Deke I knew it! Come on, Brett - get it off your chest.

Brett Okay, Mr Brenton, I won't beat around the b...

Deke Don't beat around the bush, Brett. Just give me the bottom line.

Brett I've been offered another job, and I've decided to accept.

Deke I see. Is there anything I can say to make you reconsider?

Brett I really don't think so, Mr Brenton, I'm sorry.

Deke Look, Brett, you're the best...

Brett I'm the only...

Deke You're the only goddam copywriter I've got. And I'm not going to let you go without a fight.

He suddenly attacks him.

Brett Argh! Mr Brenton, please - no!

Deke (*recovering his composure*) So, you'll be leaving us then.

Brett I'm afraid so, Mr Brenton.

Deke How much?

Brett What?

Deke How much are they paying you?

Brett Oh, Mr Brenton, it's not the money...

Deke I'll double it.

Brett I'll stay.

Deke Good. Now, who was it? Who offered you the job?

Brett Oh, I'm not really sure I should say, Mr Brenton.

Deke Come on, Brett, or I'll squeeze your nuts so hard your eyes will pop out.

Brett Well, when you put it like that...I had this letter - just out of the blue, from a big agency down-town. It's crazy - I've never even met the woman.

A Flying Ducks Publication

Deke Woman?
Brett She signed herself "Lana".

Deke recoils in horror.

Deke The bitch. She never gives in, does she.
Brett You know her?
Deke It's my wife.
Brett Your wife?
Deke She's out to wreck my company, Brett. She's stolen every good man I ever had - every good account I ever had. But not this time. She's not getting her hands on my best copywriter - and she's not getting her sticky little fingers on my Friends condoms. This company was built on the sweat of my Grand-daddy, Brett. And I'm not having it ripped from under my nose by some no-good two-bit gold-digging whore!
Brett I take it you and Lana don't get along.
Deke Don't ever...ever mention that name in this office again. Understood?
Brett You mean Lana?
Deke Yes, Lana!
Brett Whatever you say, Mr Brenton.
Deke (*with an almost schizophrenic change of mood*) Are you happy here, Brett?
Brett Delirious, Mr Brenton.
Deke Some people say I'm too...autocratic. You don't think I'm too autocratic, do you, Brett?
Brett No, sir.
Deke (*friendly*) Sit down. Stand up. Do a twirl. Good to have you aboard again, Brett.
Brett Thank you, Mr Brenton.
Deke Call me Deke.
Brett Thank you, Mr Deke.
Deke Okay. Let's go. Let's get to work on this new campaign.

Brett goes to leave with the papers. Deke calls him back, holding up a packet of Friends condoms.

Deke Hey, Brett. You ever used one of these things?
Brett Er, shucks, no, Mr Brenton.
Deke Well how the hell do you expect to write about them if you've never tried them? Go on, enjoy yourself. Get to know the product.

A Flying Ducks Publication

Brett Thanks, Mr Brenton...er...Deke!

He goes to leave, clutching his condom packet enthusiastically. Enter Foxglove. Brett immediately hides the condom packet behind his back, embarrassed. Foxglove talks in a childish sing-song voice, and drags one leg pathetically behind her, like Tiny Tim from "A Christmas Carol".

Foxy Hello, daddy!
Deke (*unenthusiastic*) Hello, Foxy. (*Mumbling*) Brett, this is my daughter, Foxglove.
Brett What?
Deke (*shouting angrily*) I said this is my daughter, Foxglove! Foxy, this is my copywriter, Brett Howard.
Foxy Hello.
Brett Hello, Foxglove.
Foxy (*feeling his jumper*) New jersey?
Brett Baltimore.
Foxy (*bemused*) Oh. What have you got behind your back?
Brett Er...nothing.
Foxy Is it something for me?
Brett Maybe...
Deke Shut it, Brett.
Foxy Daddy - look what Foxy's got!

She shows him an opened cigar box.

Deke Another pet, huh?
Foxy Yeah! This is Mousey Wousey.
Deke Well, just make sure Mousey Wousey don't crap on my carpet. Remember what happened to little Fluffy Wuffs.
Foxy Okay, daddy. Say hello to Mousey Wousey, Brett.
Brett Er, hi there, little fellah!
Foxy Isn't he cute?
Brett You keep him in a *ceegar* box?
Foxy Sure - he likes it!
Brett But he could suffocate in there.
Foxy I don't care.

Brett sidles over to Deke, with a cheesy grin.

A Flying Ducks Publication

Brett Forgive me for asking like this, Mr Brenton. But is your daughter one brick short of a load?

Deke Let me tell you, Brett. Foxy was the brightest, fittest girl in college. At eight years old she could run like the wind. At eleven she took on thirty chess grand masters all at once.

Brett Wow!

Deke She lost every game. But she was a special kind of kid, Brett. Then, it happened.

Brett What?

Deke The day Lana and I split up, she turned into a dithering idiot with a limp.

Brett That's terrible.

Deke That was just the beginning. Then came the fight for custody of the kid. We dragged Foxy through every law court in Chicago. Like two wild animals fighting over a piece of meat. And all the time I knew we were tearing her apart, inside. But I wouldn't give up. And neither would Lana. On the day of the final hearing I stood in court, and looked across at my little girl. She smiled. There was a lump in my throat as big as a baseball. Brenton versus Brenton. The lives of three people about to be decided by some white-haired judge who didn't give a damn.

Brett What happened?

Deke I lost.

Brett She lives with her mother.

Deke No, she lives with me. God damn that judge.

Brett That's a sad story, Mr Brenton.

Deke We've tried every doctor in Chicago.

Brett It's not doctors she needs, Mr Brenton. It's love. The love of a good man. And the love of her pa-*rents*.

Enter Lana, glamorous rich-bitch wife of Deke Brenton. Her shoulder pads are so wide, she has to turn sideways to get through the door. Lana is English born.

Lana How touching.

Deke Lana! What the hell do you want?

Foxy Momma!

Lana Hello, Foxglove.

Foxy This is Mousey Wousey!

Lana I'll say hello to Mousey Wousey later, honey. Now go and play outside for a moment while I talk to your father.

Foxy Okay.

A Flying Ducks Publication

Lana takes the cigar box from Foxy and places it on Deke's desk. Foxy exits.

Lana Deke, love of my life. How's business?

Deke Business is fine. No thanks to you.

Lana Gone a little downhill, haven't you, darling? I can remember when you had a desk like a football pitch.

Deke I got fed up with cutting the grass. Now say what you came here to say and get out. I'm a busy man.

Lana You must be Brett Howard.

Brett Yes ma'am.

Lana I was expecting a younger man.

Brett You should have come earlier.

Lana Witty too. We're going to get along just fine. Are you all packed?

Deke I think Brett's got something to tell you, Lana.

Brett Erm, I've decided to stay here, Mrs Brenton.

Deke Hah!

Lana How much?

Brett What?

Lana How much did he offer you?

Brett Oh, it's not just the money, Mrs Brenton...

Lana I'll triple it.

Brett I'm all yours.

Deke Goddammit, Lana! That means he'll be earning nearly five thousand dollars a week!

Lana Is that all? Let's make it ten thousand.

Deke You're not beating me this time, Lana. Twelve thousand.

Lana Fifteen.

Deke Twenty.

Lana Twenty-five.

Brett looks anxiously on, and encourages Deke to continue.

Brett Come on!

Deke Fifty thousand dollars a week.

Brett Wow!

Lana A hundred thousand.

Deke Five hundred thousand. (*No response from Lana*) What's the matter, Lana? Lost your bottle?

Lana (*producing a small bottle*) It's right here, Deke. Seven hundred and fifty thousand.

Deke One million dollars.

Brett With you then, sir, at one million dollars. Any more? All done then, at one million dollars a week....(*he bangs the table to close the sale*)... Mr Brenton. (*Deke knees Brett in the nuts*) Uggh! What was that for?

Deke If I'm going to pay you one million dollars a week, you're going to sweat for it. You'll get one of those every hour, on the hour.

Enter Foxy.

Deke I've won, Lana. I've beaten you!

Lana Take him. He's no good to me now, anyway.

Foxy Momma....

Lana pushes Foxy aside - the palm of her hand to Foxy's face - and makes for the door. She is halted by Brett's angry call.

Brett Mrs Brenton! Why do you and Mr Brenton have to keep feuding like this? It's hard on poor little Foxy. It really is!

Lana (*angrily*) Let me tell you something, Brett Howard. A long time ago, Deke and I loved each other very much indeed. I'd have done anything for him. Until I found him in bed with that...that old cow!

Deke You leave Daisy out of this!

Brett Daisy?!?

Lana Oh, hasn't he told you? I thought maybe he'd have introduced you to some of his farm animal friends.

Deke Lana - not in front of the kid!

Lana She's a dithering idiot with a limp, Deke. She doesn't understand a word we're saying - do you Foxglove?

Foxy No, momma.

Deke Look, this was all a long time ago. I'm a different man now.

Lana You disgust me!

Deke At least Daisy listened to me - which is more than you ever did.

Lana Is that why you gave her a job?

Brett A job?

Lana As his secretary. Didn't you know?

Brett You took on a cow??

Deke She's a good worker!

Lana Hah!

Brett Can she type?

Deke Oh come on, Brett! She has cloven hooves for Christ's sake!

Lana See what I mean? You're working for a pervert.

Deke After ten years married to you, Lana, even a cow starts to look attractive.

Lana All I can say is, the cow must have been particularly desperate.

Deke You know, the thing I resent most about you Lana is that you never gave me a son to take over this business.

Brett (*covering Foxy's ears*) For pity's sake, Mr Brenton...

Lana And what did your other lover give you - a heffer?

Deke That's below the belt, Lana, and you know it.

Lana And what do you call blaming me for not giving you a son? I can't believe you held it against me.

Deke You know damn well I held it against you every night for a month, and nothing happened.

Lana You always were stupid, Deke.

Deke Get out, Lana. And don't ever come back. (*Deke reaches for a cigar from the cigar box. He inadvertently grabs the mouse, bites its head off, and is about to light it*) Goddammit! What's this??

He spits the head out, and holds the body aloft by the tail. Foxy screams hysterically.

Foxy Arrrgh! Mousey Wousey!!!

Lana Now see what you've done!

Deke Get her out of here, Brett!

Brett Yes, sir. Come along, Foxy. He's only bitten the head off. We can soon fix him up.

He takes the screaming Foxy out.

Deke All right Lana - you've said your piece, now get out.

Lana It will be a pleasure. (*She goes to leave, and turns*) Oh, I knew there was something else I had to tell you. I've just been on the phone to the Chairman of Friends Condom Corporation. You've lost the account. He's given it to me.

Deke You?

Lana I persuaded him that if he wanted to see some real growth in condoms, he should let a woman handle it.

Deke I've lost the whole account?

Lana The whole shooting match.

Deke I'm ruined.

A Flying Ducks Publication

Lana Oh, that was just for starters, Deke. Get this. As soon as I telephoned round your shareholders and broke the news, they were practically falling over themselves to sell me shares on the cheap. I now own fifty-one percent of Brenton & Brenton stock.

Deke What?

Lana I'm the new owner, Deke. And I'm giving you exactly two hours to get out of my office.

Exit Lana to dramatic music. Deke, still spitting mouse hair, reaches for the intercom.

Deke Get Matt Kirby on the phone - I want to see him right away.

A "mooooo!" comes from the intercom. Enter immediately Matt Kirby, a well-dressed English lawyer. His delivery is dry and laconic.

Matt I came as soon as I could, Deke.

Deke Matt, come in. Help yourself to coffee.

Matt Thanks. (*He puts the coffee jar in his briefcase*)

Deke So. How's the best Attorney in the business?

Matt Fine.

Deke And how are you?

Matt I'm fine too. What can I do for you, Deke? Your secretary sounded pretty agitated on the phone.

Deke She probably needs milking.

Matt What?

Deke Never mind. Matt, I want a divorce.

Matt Who from?

Deke From my wife.

Matt On what grounds?

Deke Right here will do fine.

Matt No, I mean what are your reasons?

Deke I hate her guts, she hates mine.

Matt Come on, Deke. You'll need to do better than that.

Deke She's taking over my company.

Matt Money! Now we're cooking! I'll need all the facts. When did you last have sex?

Deke What the hell's that got to do with it?

Matt Nothing. I just love it when you talk dirty.

Deke Matt, we haven't kissed in over a year.

Matt I know but we're still friends aren't we?

Deke No, I mean Lana and me. I can't even remember when we last held hands.

Matt What about intercourse?

Deke No thanks, Matt. I've got a headache.

Matt Pity. But I meant Lana and you. When did you last have intercourse with your wife?

Deke We did that last night. But it wasn't the same, Matt. When Lana and I first met, it was like dynamite. For the first half an hour of our marriage we made love every twenty minutes. On the sofa. On the hearth rug. In the car. Up the stairs. In the microwave. In the dishwasher. In the dog's kennel. In the hamster's cage....

Matt In bed...

Deke Don't be disgusting, Matt.

Matt And now it's all over.

Deke That's right.

Matt Is there another woman involved?

Deke I don't think so. Lana's heterosexual.

Matt No, I meant with you.

Deke Me? No way. Not another woman.

Matt Another man?

Deke No.

Matt What then? (*Deke hesitates*) Come on, Deke. If I'm going to represent you I need to know everything.

Deke Well, I did have an affair...with a farm animal.

Matt I don't need to know this.

Deke It was a female farm animal.

Matt Thank God for that. For a moment there I thought you'd gone queer on me.

Deke I can't afford any scandal on this one, Matt. I'm a respectable businessman.

Matt No you're not - you're in advertising.

Deke So, will you represent me?

Matt There's a problem, Deke. It's Lana. Don't forget I am her brother.

Deke That's why I chose you, Matt. I knew you more than anyone would know how her mind worked.

Matt Mmm. There is another problem, Deke. It's Lana again. Don't forget I'm also her lawyer.

Deke So?

Matt So, I'd have to represent both of you.

A Flying Ducks Publication

Deke And if I file for divorce?
Matt I'll advise her to fight it.
Deke Then what would you advise me to do?
Matt I'll advise you not to take any of that nonsense. Keep pushing for divorce.
Deke And then?
Matt I'd advise her to take you for every penny you've got. You can see my problem, Deke. I can't represent you. It's unethical.
Deke Matt. I'm telling you. If I don't get a divorce I'm going to kill her!

Brett goes to enter, overhears the conversation, and lingers unseen in the doorway, listening.

Matt Murder? Now we're talking. What can I do to help?
Deke Matt, I want you to hire me a hit man!
Matt A what man?
Deke You heard me.
Matt Now hold on just a cotton-picking moment. You don't just look up hit men under "H" in the Yellow Pages you know.
Deke No, but when you've been around the Chicago streets as long as I have, you get to know the codes. (*He grabs a magazine*) Look, in the personal column of this magazine. "Caravan for sale. Sixth berth. Good condition."
Matt So what?
Deke So what? That's a mob code, Matt. It means, "Hit man for hire".
Matt You're pulling my leg.
Deke I'm telling you, Matt. This guy is an assassin. Six berth, too - that means he's good. You've got to know the codes.
Matt What magazine is that?
Deke (*checking the front cover*) Hit Man Monthly.
Matt Okay, Deke. I'll give it a try. We'll blow that little bitch out of the water.
Deke Get to it, Matt. And keep me posted. If Lana so much as scratches her leg, I want to know about it.
Matt Right.

Exit Matt. Deke takes a cigar, and bites off the end.

Deke Ok, Lana - first round to you. But when I've finished with you, you're going to wish you'd never been born. I just need a few days.

Lights fade. Exit Deke. Matt enters in a spotlight, to deliver a short narration.

A Flying Ducks Publication

Matt "But the days turned to weeks, and the weeks turned to months, and time was not kind to Deke Brenton. He began to drink heavily. He began to gamble heavily. With most of his vast wealth tied up in Brenton & Brenton stock, Deke soon had to sell his luxury home to pay for his twilight existence, and he sent Foxy to live in a broom cupboard in the agency. For the first time in his life, Deke Brenton knew what it was like to be poor and, still obsessed with killing Lana, he continued his desperate search for a hit man who would accept one of the major credit cards. Meanwhile, Lana Brenton was beginning to wonder whether gaining single-handed control of Chicago's biggest ad agency was a victory, or a punishment..."

Exit Matt. Full lights up to reveal Lana entering the room, on a cordless phone. She moves towards the desk.

Lana I'm sorry, Frank, you just can't ignore the research figures. Ninety-five percent of all women were against the idea. No, I am not being negative. I just don't think the market is ready for a scratch-and-sniff condom just yet. Let's just wait to see how the matching condom and duvet range goes down first, okay? (*She slams down the phone, picks up another phone and punches in a short number*) Brett. Where are those figures I asked you for?

Brett (*entering immediately, talking into yet another cordless phone*) They're right here, Mrs Brenton. (*He produces two little figurines*)

Lana Put them on my desk. (*A phone rings. Lana tries three different hand-sets before tracking down the right one*) Hello? Hello? Hello? Yes, Frank. Are you sure? Right, okay Frank. I owe you a pint!

Brett Good news?

Lana No. He just phoned to tell me I owe him a pint. Look Brett - I'm not paying you to hang around here gossiping - haven't you got work to do?

Brett (*offended, but proud*) Sure. (*He goes to exit*)

Lana Brett, stop. Look, I'm sorry if I've been snapping at you lately, I'm under a lot of pressure.

Brett I'm used to it.

Lana Well, I'm not. In a crazy sort of way I miss Deke. He used to handle all the business side of things. I was just the ideas woman. His inspiration - that's what he used to call me.

Brett How did you two ever meet?

Lana Oh, it's a long story. A young English girl. Her first holiday abroad. Her first taste of freedom and adventure. Deke seemed to represent everything I'd ever dreamt about. Power. Wealth. Hairy chest. I'll never forget the first day.

It was at a garden party in New York. I'd got a job serving drinks. Suddenly there was a murmur of excitement, and Deke made a spectacular arrival in his helicopter. I offered him a drink, and we got talking. He was so sweet. He made me take off my working apron, and join him as his special guest. Two hours later, I was riding on his chopper. Pass me a cigarette, would you?

She takes a cigarette from the cigarette box, masked by Brett. Brett snaps the box shut.

Brett Do you think you and Mr Brenton will ever get back together again?
Lana You really know how to hurt a woman, don't you, Brett?
Brett I'm sorry. Have I said the wrong thing?
Lana No, you just shut that cigarette case on my nipple.
Brett I'm sorry.

Enter Foxy. Her progress across the stage is slow and tortuous. She delivers her line as she finally reaches Lana.

Foxy Hi, momma.
Lana Not now, Foxy, I'm busy.

Foxy instantly turns and starts the long journey back. She is used to such rebuffs and shows no hint of emotion - just the pain of movement.

Brett You shouldn't snap at her like that, Mrs Brenton. She needs all the love she can get.
Lana I'm sorry, Foxy - what is it?

Foxy, almost at the door, turns again and comes back.

Foxy Well, I'm kinda worried about daddy. He's been acting kinda strange lately.
Lana Kinda strange, eh? What kinda strange?
Foxy Well, it's kinda difficult to explain.
Lana Kinda try, honey.
Foxy Well, he's been mixing with some kinda odd characters.
Lana Like who?
Foxy I only heard him refer to them by their nicknames. Let me see, there was Mac the Knife. Frenchy the Jackal. Oh, and Eddie, the Completely Wild Sadistical Bastard.

A Flying Ducks Publication

Lana This... Eddie, the Completely Wild Sadistical Bastard. What sort of a guy was he?

Foxy He seemed pleasant enough. But he must be a mean character - why else would they call him that awful name?

Lana Oh, Eddie's not such a bad name.

Brett Look, Mrs Brenton...

Lana Call me Lana.

Brett Lana, I think these guys are hit men. I think Mr Brenton is trying to kill you.

Lana Hah! That's ridiculous. Whatever makes you think that?

Brett It's just something I overheard. Mr Brenton was talking to some guy, and he said "I'm going to kill her. I want you to find me a hit man." It probably means nothing.

Foxy There's something else, momma.

Lana What is it, honey?

Foxy Why have I got to marry that man?

Lana What man?

Foxy The friend of daddy's.

Lana Daddy says you've got to marry someone?

Foxy The man with the scar. But I don't like him, momma. Make him go away.

Lana Something smells rotten.

Brett It's probably sweat. This whole company's built on it.

Lana Deke's scheming. Brett, I want you to get him in here. Use any excuse. Just find out what he's up to.

Brett Right.

Exit Brett.

Foxy Momma?

Lana Yes, darling. What is it?

Foxy There's something I've been meaning to ask you.

Lana Fire away, honey.

Foxy Well, it's kinda personal.

Lana Would you prefer I left the room?

Foxy No, it's just that, well, I've been living in the same house as you for twenty-five years - all my life - and in that time I've never once known you go to the toilet.

Lana (*tearful*) Running an ad agency is a very demanding business, Foxy. I haven't always had the time to do the things I want. Your father and I both had

to make sacrifices so that you'd never know hardship.
Foxy When are you and daddy going to be friends again, momma?

The question is highly charged with mock emotion. Both Lana and Foxy are in tears. Emotive music gently swells underneath to heighten the deliberate tear-jerker.

Lana I don't know, darling.
Foxy Daddy doesn't care about me any more, does he, momma?
Lana Oh, Foxy, how can you say such a thing?
Foxy He's ashamed of me because I'm not like other children.
Lana No, Foxy!
Foxy It's because of me that you and daddy broke up, isn't it, momma?
Lana No, darling, no!
Foxy It is! Daddy wanted a boy and now he's going to get rid of me by making me marry the man with the scar!
Lana No, Foxy, no!!! (*She hugs Foxy very hard to her chest*) You're not going to marry anyone you don't want to, Foxy. I swear it!
Foxy (*muffled*) Momma?
Lana Yes, darling?
Foxy You're suffocating me, momma.

Lana lets go, and Foxy collapses to the floor.

Lana What are you up to, Deke? What the hell are you up to?? (*She reaches for her intercom*) Brett, get in here.

Enter Brett instantly. Foxy lies dazed on the floor.

Alice You sent for me, Mrs Brenton?
Lana Did I? Oh, yes. Any sign of Deke yet?
Brett No. I've checked every motel in the area.
Lana What about this Eddie character?
Brett I, erm, I don't think Foxy should hear this.

Lana reaches for a soda syphon and squirts it unceremoniously into Foxy's face, rousing her.

Lana Get lost, honey.
Foxy Yes, momma.

A Flying Ducks Publication

She limps away.

Lana Okay, Brett, give me the bottom line.

Brett Eddie Marango - otherwise known as Eddie, the Completely Wild Sadistical Bastard - was released from Chicago State Prison last week. Sorry, Mrs Brenton. I was right. He's a hit man. The best in the country. And the most expensive.

Lana Damn. Still, there's one comforting thought. Most of Deke's money is tied up in Brenton & Brenton stock. There's no way he could raise the cash to pay for a top hit man.

Brett According to *po*-leece records, Eddie is licensed to accept most of the major credit cards.

Lana You really know how to cheer a girl up, don't you, Brett? Okay - get out of here. Keep searching.

Brett Right.

Exit Brett.   Lana gets a revolver from her desk drawer.   She examines it apprehensively. Enter Blanche De-Ville.

Blanche So it was you who shot JR.

Lana (*spinning round*) Who are you?

Blanche Never mind. It's not you I want to see - it's Deke.

Lana (*putting the revolver back into the desk drawer*) Deke's not here.

Blanche I'll wait.

Lana No you won't. What the hell do you want?

Blanche Relax. This is none of your business.

Lana On the contrary. This is all my business. This happens to be my office. And Deke happens to be my husband.

Blanche Don't lecture me, darling. Deke and I were lovers long before you knew which end to put your lipstick on. By the way, I think you chose the wrong end.

Lana Be careful, darling, or I might punch one of your chins.

Blanche Well, well. The English Rose has a few thorns.

Lana Get out of here before I call security.

Blanche Don't get so twitchy. I'm Blanche De-Ville.

Lana Blanche De-Ville! Deke's first wife!

Blanche I'm flattered you've heard of me.

Lana At least now I can see why he traded you in for a younger model.

Blanche Younger, maybe. But certainly no model.

Lana Give the lady a saucer of milk. So what are you up to, Blanche? Come back to try and steal my man?

Blanche Darling, a warthog could steal your man.

Lana Oh, then you won't have any trouble, will you?

Blanche Save your breath. I'm not interested in Deke.

Lana Join the club.

Blanche Oh - you two had a little lovers' tiff?

Lana You could say that. I've ruined him and thrown him out onto the streets.

Blanche I'm impressed. That's exactly what Deke did to me.

Lana It's not like him to show such good taste. What happened?

Blanche (*the hard exterior melodramatically dissolves into tears*) He never forgave me for losing our baby son.

Lana (*regretful*) I'm sorry. I had no idea. Maybe we have more in common that you'd imagine. Deke's never forgiven me for not bearing him a son. He resents our only daughter, Foxy.

Blanche The dithering idiot with a limp?

Lana You've met her?

Blanche She was in reception.

Lana She wasn't making a nuisance of herself, was she?

Blanche No, she was playing quietly up the corner with a headless mouse.

Lana Bless her.

Blanche You must be very proud of her.

Lana Er...yes. Look, Blanche. Why did you come here? Is it money you want?

Blanche Money will never bring back my son.

Lana No, but it buys a lot of distractions.

Blanche Forget it. Besides, I've found myself another husband. And he's rolling in the stuff.

Lana So what's the deal?

Blanche It's Deke's forgiveness I need. I can't go on living with the guilt.

Lana You must stop blaming yourself. That's what Deke does to you. He twists your mind.

Blanche Maybe you're right. I'd just like to hear it from Deke. We were so happy before...it...happened. Deke was devastated.

Lana Maybe he has something to thank you for. He channelled all that screwed up emotion into his business, and ruthlessly built the biggest agency in Chicago. Nothing else mattered to Deke.

Blanche But at least he has Foxy.

Lana (*flatly*) Yes. I never had the heart to tell Deke that he wasn't the real father.

Blanche What?

Lana That would have been the last straw.

Blanche Does Foxy know?

Lana Of course not. It would kill her. She worships the ground Deke walks on.
And he treats her like a...like a...dithering idiot with a limp.

Blanche So who was the father?

Lana Oh, it was just a casual affair with a travelling brush salesman.

Blanche Tall guy? Blond hair and glasses?

Lana You know him?

Blanche I married him. That travelling brush salesman now owns the biggest
direct selling company in the world.

Lana Well I never. I'm sorry.

Blanche Oh, don't be. No doubt he offered to demonstrate that brush for
smoothing out unwanted body hair.

Lana Yes.

Blanche Never fails.

Lana We have a lot to talk about. Come on. I'll buy you lunch.

Blanche Lead the way.

Exit Lana and Blanche through one door, as Foxy enters through another.

Foxy Momma? Where are you, momma?

She looks around at the empty office, and sits patiently at the desk. Enter Brett.

Brett Lana, here's the copy for the new TV campaign you asked...hello, Foxy.
What are you doing here?

Foxy Waiting for momma.

Brett Haven't you got a home to go to?

Foxy No. I live in the broom cupboard on the second floor.

Brett You do what?

Foxy Daddy sent me there.

Brett He's thrown you out?

Foxy He had to sell the house.

Brett Does your momma know you're here?

Foxy Sure. She promised to take me to lunch today. It's my birthday.

*We hear a car drive off. Brett peeks through the blind - his expression reveals he's
just seen Lana drive off.*

A Flying Ducks Publication

Brett Foxy, I think momma may have *for*-gotten.

Foxy Oh, she wouldn't do that. This is my special treat!

Brett Look, Foxy, I'm taking you to a restaurant right now, okay? Now you take the *eele*vator and wait for me downstairs. I've just got to make a *teele*phone call, okay?

Foxy Okay. (*Foxy pauses at the door, and turns*) Brett.

Brett Yeah?

Foxy Thank you.

Exit Foxy. Brett wipes away a tear, and begins to dial.

Brett Hello - is that the Child Welfare Group?

Enter Matt. Brett slams down the phone.

Matt Lana!

Brett Do I look like Lana?

Matt Where is she?

Brett Out.

Matt Don't mess around. This is urgent. I need to talk to her.

Brett You're the guy I saw with Deke. You're the guy who's plotting to kill her.

Matt Don't be ridiculous. I'm Lana's brother.

Brett Her brother?

Matt She's my sister.

Brett Your sister?

Matt Are you going to stand there repeating everything I say?

Brett Everything you say?

Matt Has Lana got a car phone?

Brett She's got three.

Matt Get her - now!

Brett (*punching in a ridiculously short number*) Damn. It's her portable answering machine. I'll try one of the other extensions. (*He does*) It's ringing. Mrs Brenton?

Matt (*snatching the phone*) Lana, it's Matt. I'm at your office. I need to see you. Now. Well turn around. It's important. And look out. There are reporters everywhere. (*He puts the phone down*)

Brett What's going on?

Matt What I have to say is for Lana's ears only. I'm going to try to head off the reporters. Which way will she come in?

Brett That way.

Brett points to one of two doors. Matt exits through it, and Lana immediately enters through the other one.

Lana (*shouting behind her*) I have no statement to make, gentlemen. I suggest you talk to my lawyers. No comment! (*She slams the door behind her*) Brett, you've got to get these newspapers off my back.

Brett rips some newspapers off Lana's back, and reads the headlines.

Brett "Gold-Digging Wife Ousts Billionaire Boss"..."Domestic Feud Wrecks Top Agency" Where are they getting all this stuff?
Lana Where do you think? Deke's running a smear campaign to discredit me. He doesn't want me to get any sympathy when I'm murdered.
Brett Can't you sue him?
Lana The one thing we don't need right now is any more publicity. Besides, when I've finished with him he'll have no money left worth suing for. Oh, God, how did we ever get into this mess?

Enter Matt, hurriedly.

Matt Lana, can we talk alone?
Lana Sure, how much do you want to borrow?
Matt No, I mean, can we talk? Alone. (*He nods his head towards Brett*)
Lana I've got no secrets from Brett. Whatever you have to say to me, you say to him too.
Matt Very well. (*He repeats each phrase, once for Lana, once for Brett*). I've been talking to Deke. I've been talking to Deke. And he's instructed me...and he's instructed me...
Lana All right, Matt. Just say it to me. Brett can listen in.
Matt Okay, Lana. It's like this...

Enter Foxy.

Foxy Brett!
Brett Shit! Sorry Foxy, I *for*-got.
Lana Oh, go and play on the freeway, will you honey? Momma's busy.
Foxy Okay.

Brett No! You stay right here, Foxy. Momma was just kidding.
Lana No I wasn't. Carry on, Matt.
Matt (*he hands Lana a piece of paper*) Deke's filing for divorce.
Foxy (*cry of anguish*) Momma!

There's a burst of melodramatic music. Foxy now has two limps. As she makes her way to Lana, she dramatically collapses.

Lana Quick - get a doctor!
Brett It's not doctors she needs, Mrs Brenton. It's love. The love of a good man, and the love of her pa-*rents*.

Brett rushes to lift Foxy up. He cradles her in his arms and carries her outside. Foxy is wailing hysterically. Brett re-enters immediately, and at that precise moment the wailing stops.

Lana How is she?
Brett She's sleeping. That was a nasty shock. Any hope of *ree*-covery has been shattered.
Matt I'm sorry, Lana. I was just doing my job.
Lana It's not your fault, Matt. You were just doing your job.
Brett We've been trying to trace Deke. Where is he?
Matt I don't know. I haven't seen him for three weeks. I receive all my instructions by post.
Brett We've heard he's hit hard times since losing the agency.
Matt It's true. He never even puts a stamp on his letters. He lost half his fortune in one night on a drunken gambling spree.
Brett Wow! Well, at least he can live off the other half.
Matt No, I'm taking that in legal fees. He's a broken man, Lana.
Lana Matt, do you know a man called Eddie?
Matt You mean Eddie, the Completely Wild Sadistical Bastard?
Lana So you do know him?
Matt Sure. He's an assassin. Deke tried to hire him because he wanted to murder his wife...ooops!
Lana It's all right, Matt - you were just doing your job.
Matt (*breaking down*) I'm sorry, Lana. I didn't realise what I was getting into. Deke showed me this magazine. There was an ad in the personal column. Like a fool I agreed to act on his behalf. I dialled the number, and...
Brett You hired him a hit man!

Matt No, I bought him a caravan.

Brett What?

Matt It was an ad for a caravan - six berth - good condition though.

Lana So where does Eddie fit into all of this?

Matt Well, when I told Deke, he threw me out of his office - he said he'd find his own hit man. A few days later, he introduced me to Eddie, the Completely Wild Sadistical Bastard.

Lana This Eddie - does he have a scar?

Matt He has a scar on his face as long as my arm.

Brett He's got a hell of a cheek.

Lana What do you know about a marriage between Eddie and my daughter?

Matt Marriage? That's crazy. Wait! Maybe it makes sense after all. No, it couldn't be true. Or could it? No. Maybe. Maybe not. Perhaps. Perhaps not...

Lana (*frustrated scream*) What??

Matt Well, I know Deke hasn't got enough money to pay for a hit man and, well, Foxy's a good-looking girl...

Lana Oh my God, no!

Matt Yup, I reckon this time Deke's sunk lower than a hedgehog's nuts.

Brett Cute expression, Matt.

The telephone rings, Lana answers it.

Lana Yes? Thank you. Well, it seems Mohammed has come to the mountain. He's in reception.

Brett Who, Mohammed?

Lana Deke, you idiot.

Lana gets the gun from her desk.

Brett What are you doing?

Matt It's all right, Brett - it's just a gun.

Brett This isn't going to solve anything. Let me talk to him, alone. Maybe I can get to the truth.

Lana All right. You've got five minutes. (*To the intercom*) Send him in.

A "moooo!" replies via the intercom. Brett looks surprised.

Lana She is a good worker. Come on, Matt.

A Flying Ducks Publication

Exit Lana and Matt. Brett waits apprehensively. A few moments later, Deke enters. He looks like a tramp, and is swigging at a whiskey bottle.

Deke Hello, Brett.

Brett Deke. You're....er...looking good.

Deke Thanks. I kinda miss the old office, you know. This was virtually my home for ten years.

Brett You know, Deke, you had another home - at home. There were two people there that cared for you very much.

Deke Yeah. Well that's all in the past.

Brett Where are you living now?

Deke I've got a caravan out of town. Six berth. Good condition though. Where's Lana?

Brett Oh, you know how it is - meetings, meetings, meetings. She won't be back for hours.

Deke How's er...how's...(*he mumbles*)

Brett What was that?

Deke (*embarrassed anger*) I said how's Foxy!

Brett Not good, Deke. She *co*-lapsed when she heard about the *dee*-vorce.

Deke Oh, God.

Brett Don't you think this feud between you two has gone far enough? It's not just your own lives you're *dee*-stroying. Every night, I watch Foxy clutch the edge of her pillow till her knuckles turn white, and cry herself to sleep, because no-one gives a damn.

Deke Is she still a dithering idiot with a limp?

Brett She's a dithering idiot with two limps. And she's scared, Deke. Scared that her daddy's going to give her away to a man with a scar like... like... like... like some piece of garbage!

Deke I don't know what...what...what...what you're talking about.

Brett And I think you're a *lee*-ar!

Deke (*banging the desk*) Goddammit, Brett. No-one calls me a *lee*-ar!

Brett (*banging the desk*) Goddammit, Deke. I'll say my piece!

Deke All right! All right. I guess I owe you an explanation. It's a long story, Brett.

Brett I'm waiting.

Deke I hired a hit man to bump off Lana and Foxy's his payment. (*Pause*) Well, maybe it wasn't such a long story after all.

Brett You hired a hit man to kill your wife and paid him with your daughter?

Deke That's right. I guess that doesn't make me much of a family man, does it?

Brett What about Foxy's feelings?

Deke She can take it - she's broad-shouldered. Just like her momma.

Brett She still hasn't forgiven you for biting the head off her mouse.

Deke I had no choice, Brett.

Brett You could have had a mint instead.

Deke I mean about the hit man. Lana's slowly strangling me, Brett. It's her or me.

Brett *(look of inspiration)* Maybe there's another way!

Deke What other way?

Brett I dunno. Maybe there is.

Deke Look at me, Brett. I'm desperate. Please help me. Please.

Brett *(picking up the phone, and offering it to Deke)* Call off the hit man, Deke. Call him off.

Deke goes to the door, and opens it slightly. A wild axe-wielding hand is pushed through, restrained by Deke pressing on the door.

Deke The deal's off, Eddie. Go home. It's over. Go home.

The grunting Eddie calms down, drops the axe, and the hand slowly disappears. Deke closes the door and moves towards Brett.

Brett You've done the decent thing, Mr Brenton.

Deke Huh! I sell my only daughter to a hit man, I try to murder my wife, I go to bed with farm animals, and still you stand by me. Why, Brett?

Brett Because I respect you, Mr Brenton. And because I'm in love with Foxy.

Deke I knew there was something between you two. Have you taken her to bed?

Brett No, she hasn't asked me yet.

Deke Well, when you do, make sure there's still something between you, like that little Friend I gave you - you know what I mean?

Brett Yes sir, Mr Brenton.

Deke You've still got it, don't you?

Brett *(tapping his groin)* It's right here, Mr Brenton.

Deke That's my boy! You know, Brett, I've begun to look on you almost as a son.

Brett Per-*ree*-ciate it, Mr Brenton.

Deke What?

Brett Per-*ree*-ciate it.

Deke Per-*ree*-ciate it? Oh, appreciate it - you appreciate it.

Brett Surely do. But listen good, Mr Brenton. You must stop punishing Foxy for not being the boy you always wanted. She loves you, Mr Brenton. And she desper-*ate*-ly needs your love. You must learn to see her for what she is. A *woe*-man.

Deke It's hard, Brett. I just can't face the fact that she'll never play Quarterback for the Chicago Bears.

Brett You mustn't give up on her like that. Maybe one day the limps will heal. And you never know - she's got a good right arm...

Deke There's something I haven't told you, Brett. There was a boy, from my first wife. But, well, she lost him.

Brett I'm sorry.

Deke Absent-minded bitch left him on a train.

Brett A train?

Deke Yeah.

Brett Which train?

Deke Why?

Brett Which train, Mr Brenton?

Deke The three thirty-five to Baltimore. But...

Brett Oh, could it be true?

Deke What?

Brett I was raised by a family in Baltimore, Mr Brenton. They found me *a*-bandonned on a train. The three thirty-five. They named me Brett because it's all they could make out of some faded letters on the side of the ca-*ree*-cot.

Deke That didn't say Brett, Brett. It said Brenton. That was our carry cot. Your real name's Billy. You're my long lost son!!

Brett Oh, daddy!

Deke Oh, son!

Brett Oh, shit!

Deke What's the matter?

Brett What about Foxy and me?

Deke Don't worry, son. She's the daughter from my second marriage!

Brett Does that mean it's all right to do it?

Deke You can do it till the cows come home, son.

Brett Bad choice of phrase, daddy.

Deke Besides, I'm not even Foxy's real father.

Brett You're not?

Deke Lana didn't even have the guts to tell me. She thinks I don't know.

Brett How did you find out?

Deke Do you remember the Homesell account?

Brett Sure. That was a great account. I never understood why we lost it.

Deke I took the boss to lunch. He started telling me stories of his cavalier days as a travelling brush salesman. Next thing he knew, he had a plate of spaghetti on his head, and...

Enter Blanche.

Blanche Please, don't go on.
Deke Blanche, what the hell?
Blanche Hello, Deke. I had to see you. Can you ever forgive me for what I did?
Deke Forgive you? Ha! Blanche, there's someone I'd like you to meet. His name's Billy.
Blanche Billy? Billy??
Deke That's right.
Blanche Oh! I don't believe it. Thank God you're safe!

She rushes over to Brett and hugs him emotionally. Brett is bemused, and stands bolt upright.

Brett Er...who is she, daddy?
Deke Billy, this is your ma.
Brett Ma? Ma? I don't believe it!

They embrace. Enter Lana.

Lana Well, well, what a touching scene.
Deke Lana!
Lana Hello, Deke. How's tricks?

He produces a bouquet of flowers from up his sleeve, and hands it to her.

Deke Not bad.
Lana For me? What's the special occasion? What are you up to, Deke?
Deke If I were you, Lana, I'd stop buying that perfume. It stinks.
Lana It's no good trying to put me off the scent, Deke. You're scheming.
Deke Lana, there's someone I'd like you to meet.
Lana Blanche and I already know each other. We use the same brushes.
Deke I'm not talking about Blanche. I'd like you to meet my long-lost son.
Lana Your son??
Deke That's right.

A Flying Ducks Publication

Lana You're no Brenton. Brentons are rich, and ruthless. You're just a nice kid from downtown Baltimore.

Brett It's true, Mrs Brenton. I'm a Brenton.

Lana Does Foxy know?

Deke Not yet.

Lana Sooner or later, Deke, you're going to have to break it to her that the boy she believes to be Brett from Baltimore is her step-brother Billy, born a Brenton.

Deke That's not going to be easy.

Brett There's something else you should know, Mrs Brenton. We're in love.

Lana Well, I suppose you're an improvement on his last bed-partner.

Brett No, not Mr Brenton and me. I'm in love with Foxy.

Lana With Foxy?

Brett Yes.

Lana You?

Brett Yes, ma'am.

Lana But, you're a handsome young man, and she's just a dithering...

Brett No! She's a beautiful, inter-*lee*-gent young *woe*-man, Mrs Brenton. It's just that you and Mr Brenton can't see that. Because you've never taken the trouble to look. You should both be *a*-shamed of yourselves!

Exit Brett.

Blanche Billy! Come back!

Blanche exits after him.

Deke Brett! Billy! Come back. Son!

Lana Let him go, Deke. He's right. We've been so busy fighting our own war, we couldn't see the damage it's done to others. Look, what happened to us in the past - I realise now it's half my fault.

Deke No, it's half my fault.

Lana Deke, I haven't been completely honest with you. About Foxy, she's...

Deke I know.

Lana You do?

Deke When you come home night after night to a house full of brushes a guy gets suspicious.

Lana I'm so sorry, Deke. You have every right to hate me. But please don't hate Foxy. Maybe it's too late for us, Deke, but Foxy's still young. She deserves a

chance. Let's not destroy the one good thing that ever came out of our
marriage.

Deke I've missed you, Lana.

Lana I've missed you too, Deke. I'm not cut out for this business.

Deke Do you really think it's too late for us?

Lana Remember the day we met, Deke?

Deke Yeah, the disco in New Orleans.

Lana The garden party in New York.

Deke Ah yes, I remember it well. You served food.

Lana No, I served wine.

Deke And I was ill.

Lana No, you were fine.

Deke Ah yes, I remember it well.

Lana Do you remember the time you picked me up in your strong arms, kissed
me softly on the corner of my mouth, and placed me gently on your chopper?

Deke Yeah. And you said I'd never get you up on one of those things.

Lana I was young.

Deke You were beautiful. You still are, Lana.

Lana Oh, Deke!

Deke By the way, I called off the hit man. You're safe now.

Lana You did that for me? Oh, Deke! Let's turn back the clocks!

*They stare passionately into each other's eyes, as sickly romantic music builds in the
background. Enter Brett with Foxy.*

Brett I've brought someone to see you.

Deke Hello, Foxy.

Foxy Hello, daddy.

*Deke takes two tentative steps towards her, and then rushes to hug her to gushes of
tears. Brett and Lana reach for tissues and blow their noses in unison.*

Deke Foxy, I've...er...I've got you a little something. It's not much, but it's all I
could afford.

Deke gives Foxy a small gift-wrapped present. She opens it, and pulls out a mouse.

Foxy Mousey Wousey! You sellotaped his head back on!

Deke It was the least I could do.

A Flying Ducks Publication

Lana That was sweet of you, Deke.

Deke That's just for starters, Foxy. We're going to be seeing a lot more of each other. Your mother and I, well, we made a lot of mistakes, but from now on, we're going to be making our mistakes together - the three of us - just like it used to be.

Brett The four of us, Foxy. Will you marry me?

Foxy Oh, Brett. Oh, daddy!

She goes to move towards the three of them, but stumbles. There's a dramatic stab of music. Deke goes to help her, but is stopped by Brett.

Brett No! Leave her. She can do it!

Foxy I can't!

Brett You can, Foxy. I know you can!

Lana We love you, Foxy!

Brett/Lana/Deke We all love you, Foxy!!

Foxy slowly and agonizingly picks herself up and, to a great swell of romantic music, she runs to her family, with a silly knees-up style run. They hug. Matt enters, and joins the hug. Blanche runs in and hugs the whole bunch of them. The spotlight narrows on the huddle of people. They all turn to the audience and grin inanely. Music climax. Spotlight to black. Curtain.

LAST PANTO
in Little Grimley

BY DAVID TRISTRAM

STARRING
(in order of incompetence)

Joyce
Gordon
Margaret
Bernard

A Note To The Director...

Last Panto in Little Grimley is a long overdue sequel to the tremendously popular Last Tango In Little Grimley, and features the same characters as the original.

Even though this is a stand-alone story, societies who haven't yet produced **Tango** might care to check it out first. Indeed, running both plays together makes for a full and very entertaining evening.

Like its predecessor, as well as being great fun, **Last Panto** is also a tremendously practical play to produce. There are just four characters (two male, two female), there's no set to build (just a few simple props) and no complex lighting or sound effects to worry about.

So, it works beautifully on even the most modest Village Hall stage, and is also ideal for Festivals.

A Flying Ducks Publication

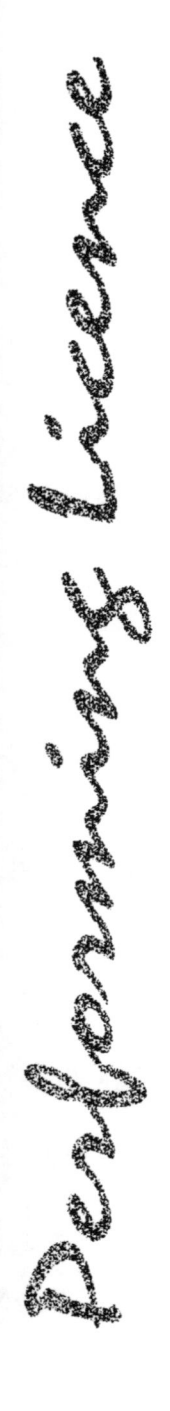
For more information on Flying Ducks Publications, write to *Flying Ducks Publications, Station Road, Highley, Shropshire* WV16 6NW.

ISBN 0 9517267 8 1

LAST PANTO IN LITTLE GRIMLEY

The scene is a simple stage, empty except for a few stage flats, stacked haphazardly in one corner. The flat on top of the ramshackle pile is a door frame, complete with opening door. None of this is in sight at first, though, as the play begins with a dramatic spotlight on Joyce, centre-stage, back to audience. She turns flamboyantly, gesturing wildly, and lets rip with her tonsils, torturing a song from a popular musical. Gordon, the harassed producer, bursts in, preferably through the audience, and onto the stage.

Gordon Joyce! Joyce.....Joyce!! (*Joyce finally relents*) How can I put this, Joyce?

Joyce How can you put what, Gordon?

Gordon Joyce, it's not going to work.

Joyce Oh, Gordon! You promised.

Gordon No, I promised I'd give it a try, Joyce, and give it a try I have, but it's not going to work.

Joyce What's the problem with it?

Gordon It's...well, it's not got the necessary...resonance, Joyce.

Joyce It's just needs the piano.

Gordon (*getting tense*) No, it does not just need the piano, Joyce. It needs the London Philharmonic orchestra, plus - and listen carefully to this bit, Joyce - it needs...some singers.

Joyce Are you trying to say that I can't sing, Gordon?

Gordon I'm not trying to say you can't sing, Joyce. I'm just trying to say that you sing in a way that is not likely to cause any pleasure.

Joyce (*highly offended*) Oh!

Gordon I've said it before, Joyce, and I'll say it again. This society is not cut out to do a musical.

Margaret has wandered in.

Margaret Call me old-fashioned, Gordon, but I thought we lived in a democracy.

Gordon This has nothing to do with politics, Margaret, this is about talent.

Margaret You know very well that Joyce went to a lot of trouble to hold a referendum in the village, and the overwhelming view was that Little Grimley wants a musical.

A Flying Ducks Publication

Gordon Joyce, how many forms did you circulate around the village?

Joyce Three hundred, Gordon.

Gordon Three hundred, Joyce. And how many replies did we have? (*A long pause*) Joyce?

Joyce Fifteen, Gordon.

Gordon Fifteen, Joyce. And of those fifteen, how many consisted of your family and immediate friends?

Joyce (*after another long, sheepish pause*) Twelve.

Gordon Twelve, Joyce.

Margaret They're still entitled to a vote, Gordon.

Gordon I know they're still entitled to a vote, Margaret. But it hardly represents a massive groundswell of opinion, does it?

Joyce I can see I'm wasting my time here. The simple fact is, Gordon, you don't don't know talent when you see it.

Gordon Well I haven't had a lot of practise, Joyce.

Joyce You just don't like musicals, do you?

Gordon (*finally snapping*) Joyce, I've tried being subtle, and now I'm going to have to put it to you straight. You sing...like a castrated pig. And you dance...like a bag of spanners. We can't do a musical, Joyce, because you're crap. Now leave it!

Joyce dissolves into shocked tears in the background, while Margaret takes Gordon to one side.

Margaret You're being too hard on her, Gordon.

Gordon It's got to be said, Margaret. If I don't hurt her feelings, the audience will. It's a simple as that.

Margaret I know what you're saying, Gordon and, believe me, I'm on your side on this one. But, well, the poor wretch.

They look round at the distraught Joyce, who's slowly collecting her coat and bag. She walks pitifully up to them.

Joyce (*snivelling*) Goodbye, Margaret. It's been nice working with you.

Margaret Joyce, don't take it personally. Gordon was only criticising your talent, not you.

Joyce (*proudly*) Gordon, I hope you find the perfectionism you're seeking.

She turns and heads off, dramatically.

A Flying Ducks Publication

Margaret Gordon?

Gordon No. I'm right on this one, Margaret.

Margaret She's been with the society a long time.

Gordon There's no room for sentimentality. A good leader sticks by his decisions. Even the tough ones. There's a principle involved here, Margaret, and it's bigger than both of us.

Margaret She's the only one who knows how to do the accounts.

Gordon instantly runs after her.

Gordon Joyce! Joyce!! Come back.

Margaret (*grandly repeating his line, mockingly*) There's a principle involved here, Margaret, and it's bigger than both of us.

Gordon eventually returns, comforting Joyce.

Gordon All I meant, Joyce, was that we should...we should stick to our strengths. We're only a small society - God knows we're getting smaller every year - we should do what we do best. Now come on, Joyce, I'm relying on you. You're a tremendous asset to the society. Please. Stick to what you do best.

Joyce (*bravely, through the snivels*) You mean...straight acting, Gordon?

Gordon (*a wide-eyed pause*) Well...erm...I meant photocopying and things, Joyce. You're so very good at that. Right, that's all settled then. Come on Joyce, take your coat off, we've got a lot to get through tonight. Look, I've even done an agenda - here it is - item one...

Margaret Point of order.

Gordon Yes, Margaret, what now?

Margaret We are not a quorum.

Gordon Where's Bernard?

Margaret He was here when I arrived. He was striking the old set.

Joyce He's probably up in the lighting box.

Gordon (*squinting into the lights and shouting*) Bernard!!

Bernard's voice comes from under the ramshackle pile of flats.

Bernard What?

Gordon Where are you?

Bernard I'm under here.

A Flying Ducks Publication

Gordon traces the voice to the flats, and opens up the door, under which Bernard is lying.

Gordon Bernard, what the hell are you doing under there? We're trying to hold a meeting.

Bernard (*still unseen*) I'm trying to recover from a severe bout of concussion.

Gordon Come on, Bernard, we haven't got time to prat about.

Gordon closes the "door" on Bernard, who then slowly clambers out, sporting a bruised forehead.

Joyce Hallo, Bernard.

Bernard Hallo, Joyce. Good evening, Margaret.

Margaret Bernard.

Bernard Do you remember this flat, Margaret?

Margaret Should I?

Bernard I think you should, Margaret. It's the one you were holding for me while I was taking the nails out of the bottom. This is the same flat, Margaret, that you then let go of.

Margaret I got sidetracked, Bernard.

Bernard I got flattened, Margaret.

Margaret Well, why didn't you just call for help if you were in trouble, instead of all this over-dramatic nonsense?

Bernard Two reasons. Two reasons, Margaret. Reason one - for the first fifteen minutes I was unconscious. And secondly, I was just curious to see how long you bastards would leave me under here without even noticing.

Margaret Art is pain, Bernard.

Bernard Too bloody right it is! Especially when it's eight foot high and smacks you on the brow.

Margaret There, you see? It only hit him on the head. It couldn't have done any real damage.

Gordon Oh, I don't know - this door frame looks a bit buckled.

Bernard Well thanks for your concern.

Gordon All right, Bernard, come on. Let's not make a crisis out of a drama.

Bernard You're lucky I'm still alive.

Margaret Matter of opinion.

Gordon All right, Margaret, don't rub salt into his head wound.

Margaret I don't know what all the fuss is about. The set's down isn't it? There you go - job done. And a damn sight quicker than normal if I might

A Flying Ducks Publication

say so.

Bernard I probably need stitches thanks to you.

Margaret The only place you need stitches, Bernard, is in that gaping gash under your nose.

Gordon (*stepping between the protagonists*) All right, all right, that's it! Sit down. Back to your corners. Both of you. End of round one.

They are ushered to seats.

Margaret End of contest, actually. I won by a knock-out.

Bernard stands to retaliate.

Gordon Leave it, Bernard! (*Handing out pieces of paper*) Let's skip item one on the agenda, shall we?

Joyce What was it?

Gordon "Suggestions for improving team spirit". Right, item two. Auditioning for possible musical. Well, I think we're all agreed on that now, aren't we?

Joyce I'm saying nothing.

Gordon Good-oh! Item three. This year's festival entry. First of all, do we really want to spend time and money entering the festival this year?

Margaret Oh, come on, Gordon. We can't not enter the festival.

Gordon Why not?

Margaret Well, it's such a prestigious event. And we didn't do too badly last year, did we, Gordon?

Gordon (*strutting about like a tense lecturer*) Let's just remind ourselves of the facts, shall we, Margaret? Fact one. Joyce's husband owns a Land Rover - a very well engineered off-road vehicle. Fact two. That was the only reason that Little Grimley Amateur Dramatic Society actually managed to make it to the festival, in one of the worst freak snow storms this country's seen in a hundred years. We were, in fact, if you recall, Margaret, the **only** society - the **only** society, Margaret - who attended the festival last year. And where were we placed overall in the competition? Third. Third, Margaret, out of one. First prize, if memory serves me, was awarded, in a hastily re-organized schedule, to the man who collects the tickets, for his owl impersonation. While second prize went to an absent society, for the best use of pauses. That adjudicator - that poor, embarrassed, beleaguered woman - could not bring herself to make us win that competition, even though we were the only ones who were there.

A Flying Ducks Publication

Margaret You're so negative, Gordon.

Gordon I am trying to be realistic, Margaret. I am trying to paint a picture - a picture of a society that desperately needs to stay within its limits. And limits. Margaret, is the one thing we have in abundance. So, what do you say? This year, let's stay away from Shakespeare, let's stay away from the festival, let's stay away from musicals, and concentrate on what we're best at.

Bernard You've written another play, haven't you, Gordon?

Gordon Well, it's funny you should say that, Bernard. It just so happens that the creative juices have been flowing again.

Margaret Are you taking minutes, Joyce?

Joyce Yes.

Margaret Right, well minute this. I am not revealing my breasts again.

Gordon You don't have to, Margaret. I do have range you know. This is an entirely different genre from my first play.

Joyce Different what?

Margaret I think he means it's not a comedy.

Bernard Look, if Margaret lobs her tits out, it's a comedy.

Gordon Shut it, Bernard.

Bernard Well, it's certainly not going to be a thriller, is it?

Margaret How would you like another stage flat on your head?

Gordon If you two could just stop bickering for one second, I might explain.

Joyce How do you spell that word?

Margaret What? Explain?

Joyce No...John something.

Gordon Genre, Joyce. J, E, N...

Margaret G, E, N.

Gordon G, E, N...erm...E...

Margaret R, E.

Gordon R, E.

Joyce (scribbling furiously) J, E, N, G, E, N, E, R, E, R, E.

Gordon Style, Joyce, just write style. In fact, don't write anything, just listen.

Joyce You're the one who told me to take minutes, Gordon. To avoid any arguments later.

Bernard Oh, come on. When have you ever known us to argue?

Gordon Look, you're going to have to keep up, Joyce. I can't keep going back over things.

Joyce I'm doing my best, Gordon.

Margaret How are the shorthand lessons coming along, Joyce?

Joyce The teacher's very pleased with me, actually. I'm up to eight words a

minute now. And my accuracy has gone up to seventy-five percent.

Bernard Great. So not only can you write eight words a minute, you can understand six of them.

Joyce That's from a standing start, Bernard. Eighteen months ago I couldn't do any of this.

Margaret Well I think it's very commendable, Joyce. Going to night school just to make our meetings more efficient.

Gordon Can we get on?

Margaret (*barbed*) Don't you think so, Gordon!

Gordon Yes, yes, thank you, Joyce. We're all eternally grateful and we don't know where we'd be without your unique skills. Now can we please attend to the business in hand?

Margaret Which is?

Gordon I've forgotten now. Where were we?

Joyce (*smugly*) It's a good job I'm taking minutes, isn't it, Gordon? Would you like me to read back the last note?

Gordon Yes, please, Joyce.

Joyce (*giving a little formal cough, and squinting at her notes*) Erm... something... something...erm...oh, yes. Style. And then Gordon said..."You're going to have to keep up, Joyce."

Gordon Is that it?

Joyce That's when you distracted me.

Gordon Something, something, style?

Joyce I'd put that other big word in, but you made me take it out again.

Bernard We were talking about your new play, Gordon.

Gordon Thank you, Bernard!

Bernard Don't mention it.

Gordon Yes, as I was trying to explain, under item four on the agenda, your chairman has turned his attentions to our next production, and as a result...

Bernard Hold on, hold on. Our **next** production?

Gordon Correct.

Bernard But our next production's the panto.

Gordon Precisely.

Margaret You've written a panto?

Gordon I've written **the** panto, Margaret.

Margaret Why?

Gordon Why not?

Margaret What's wrong with a professional pantomime script?

Gordon Nothing, Margaret. Until we get hold of it. And then we invariably

torture it, starve it of meaning, castrate it, and offer it for public consumption.

Bernard Sounds like one of our better productions.

Gordon I'd go further, Margaret. I'd say that if there were a Royal Society for the Prevention of Cruelty to Scripts, we'd be serving life.

Margaret So you're saying we should take out the only strong link in the chain.

Gordon What I'm saying, Margaret, is that a society like ours needs a custom-written script. Why? To make sure we can cast it with the people we've got. To make sure that it plays to our strengths - if we can find any. And above all, to make sure we have a complete sell-out.

Margaret Noble aims. How do you intend to achieve them?

Gordon Easy, Margaret. You see, this is a panto with a twist.

Margaret (*suspiciously*) What sort of twist?

Gordon It's a sex panto.

Margaret I don't think I heard you properly, Gordon. For a moment there I thought you said a sex panto.

Gordon I did.

Margaret (*getting up and leaving*) Good-night everyone.

Gordon Margaret! Wait! Hear me out.

Margaret Gordon, if a pantomime is anything, it's a piece of traditional family entertainment. I refuse to be part of this...perversion.

Gordon But that's where this is so clever. Come on, Margaret - let's face it. We've got a major problem with our panto. The audiences are shrinking year by year. I watched it happening. Year one - family outing, everybody excited, the kids enjoy it, mom and dad sit there bored stiff. Year two, mom takes the kids to the mid-week matinee, dad says "No thanks" and goes up the pub. Year three, mom says "Sod this for a game of soldiers, I'm not having the hassle - here's a fiver kids, go on your own". Year four, kids say "This is crap, give us the fiver, we're off to the pictures". Well, not this time, Margaret. Why? Because my panto works on two levels.

Margaret And I bet one of them is gutter level.

Gordon When are you going to learn to trust me, Margaret?

Margaret When you learn some common sense. You're playing with fire. There's a principle involved here, Gordon, and it's bigger than all of us.

Gordon Well, you're a great believer in democracy, Margaret. Why don't we put it to the people. What do you say, Bernard?

Bernard (*removing a squashed banana from his pocket*) She's flattened my banana!

Gordon And that's your last word on the matter, is it?

Bernard What?

A Flying Ducks Publication

Gordon The panto, Bernard! What about the panto?

Bernard Look, you know me. As long as it uses standard flats, and as long as I'm not in it, I don't give a stuff what we put on.

Gordon Remind me to put you on our reading committee next year, Bernard. That sort of insight is so valuable.

Bernard (*referring back to his banana*) This was my bloody tea, you know.

Gordon Joyce, you've been fairly quiet until now. What do you think? (*Joyce is scribbling furiously, and is in a world of her own*) Joyce?

Joyce (*concentrating hard*) Shhh...

Gordon Joyce!!

Joyce (*looking up*) What?

Gordon Where are you?

Joyce I'm doing all right, Gordon.

Gordon Where are you, Joyce?

Joyce Erm...the bit where you say something about torturing scripts.

Gordon Oh, Joyce!

Joyce Well, that bit slowed me down. There was a word I didn't understand.

Gordon What word, Joyce?

Joyce Castrate. I mean I know it's got something to do with the cast. And rate - that's speed, isn't it. So does it mean, like, the speed of the cast, how they read, or...what are you laughing at, Bernard?

Bernard Joyce, it means chopping off your bollo..

Gordon All right, Bernard! We don't need it in technicolour. Joyce, may I borrow your note-pad for a second. May I?

Joyce Of course, Gordon.

Gordon And the pencil. Thank you. (*He takes the note-pad and pencil, and tears out all the pages, leaving just the front and back cardboard cover. He snaps the pencil in half, and then calmly hands all the left-overs back to Joyce*) No more minutes, Joyce. They're turning into hours. Just listen. I have written this year's panto. Are you going to support me, or not?

Joyce Gordon, there's something I have to say.

Gordon Say it, Joyce.

Joyce I've been with this society for over twelve years.

Gordon I know that, Joyce.

Joyce And in that time, Gordon, I've always stuck by you, through thick and thin.

Bernard Mainly thick.

Gordon I know that, Joyce. And you'll never know how much that means to me.

Joyce And, no matter what you've said to me, Gordon, over the years, no matter
how rude you've been, I've never held a grudge.

Gordon This is true, Joyce. You never have.

Joyce Even that time, on April 14th, 1987, at twenty-five minutes to eight, when
you told me I had less talent - and I believe I'm quoting you exactly here,
Gordon - than a bucket of donkey droppings.

Gordon Heat of the moment, Joyce. We both know you're better than that.

Joyce Well, this time I think you've gone too far.

Gordon What?

Joyce The answer's no, Gordon.

Margaret Good for you, Joyce!

Gordon What?

Joyce You heard me. I said no, Gordon. Emphatically no. With a capital M.

Gordon I see. Well, that's a pity. A great pity, Joyce. Because, of course, were
we to go ahead with this project, we would need a good Musical Director.

Joyce Musical Director?

Gordon Someone with a fine voice, Joyce. Someone with an incomparable
understanding of choreography. Someone with natural rhythm. And I'd like
you, Joyce...to help us look for him.

Joyce Oh, Gordon!

Gordon Just joking, Joyce. If you want it, the job's yours. MD, Joyce.

Joyce MD?

Gordon Musical Director.

Bernard Or CP.

Joyce CP?

Bernard Castrated Pig.

Gordon You're not helping, Bernard.

Bernard Or how about DD? Donkey Droppings?

Gordon Ignore him, Joyce. He's just jealous.

Joyce I don't know, Gordon.

Gordon What does your heart tell you, Joyce?

Gordon starts humming Joyce's opening song softly into her ear, as Joyce stares into
space, daydreaming herself into glory.

Joyce I'll do it!

Gordon Good man, Joyce.

Joyce On one condition.

Gordon Name it, Joyce. The world is your oyster.

A Flying Ducks Publication

Joyce That, whatever happens, you won't lose your temper with me during rehearsals.

Gordon is momentarily stunned into silence, as he grapples with the enormity of the request.

Gordon Joyce...I...you...Joyce, we both have an enormous challenge before us. All anyone can ask, is that we both do our very best.

Joyce Very well, Gordon.

Gordon Two down, one to go. Well, Margaret, once again, it's down to you.

Margaret I think I've made my position perfectly clear, Gordon. I don't like it. You're messing around with a great tradition.

Gordon Margaret, the only tradition that this society has upheld over the years, is one of failure. If the audiences get any smaller we might as well do a door-to-door tour. Look what we're in competition with. Big-budget, professional pantos. With orchestras. Special effects. Even actors. We can't offer that. If we want a cat in hell's chance of dragging them in we've got to give them something different.

Margaret Well this is certainly different.

Gordon Yes, and proud of it, Margaret. I'm fed up of the cast outnumbering the audience. I'm fed up of ex-sportsmen and hack soap stars stealing our glory. Are we going to lie down and die? Or are we going to fight back? Come on, Margaret. Let's show Bruno the knockout blow. Let's hit Botham for six. Let's show those TV stars there's more to theatre than acting. Well?

Margaret It's traditional in pantomime for the male lead to be played by a female.

Gordon Yes, it is, Margaret.

Margaret May I assume, Gordon, that that is one tradition you will not be ditching.

Gordon You may.

Bernard Does this mean we get to see her in tights?

Gordon (*aside*) Bernard, I'm at a very delicate stage in the negotiations. Shut your trap.

Margaret Am I to be offered any editorial control over the script?

Gordon The usual clause, Margaret. On performance nights, you have my permission to leave out any lines you can't remember.

Margaret Very well.

Gordon Yes! Bravo, Margaret!

Margaret But I'd like my reservations minuted.

A Flying Ducks Publication

Gordon Later, Joyce, later. Treat it as homework. Right then, I suggest we
move onto the final item on my agenda, which is to agree a date for the first
rehearsal. Now, how's everybody fixed for next Thursday?

*Margaret has reached for her filofax, Joyce has a large desk diary, Bernard relies on
memory.*

Bernard Thursday's no good for me, I've got a plastering job in Manchester.
Gordon Wednesday, then.
Joyce Wednesday's my shorthand class, Gordon.
Gordon Well, mustn't make you miss one of those, must we, Joyce. I'd hate you
to fall behind the pace. Tuesday, then.
Margaret No, no, no. Not Tuesdays. That's my late night.
Bernard I'm all right any other Thursday.
Joyce I can't make every alternate Thursday. W.I. meetings.
Gordon Which alternate Thursday can you make?
Joyce This one coming.
Gordon That's no good for Bernard. What about Monday week?
Bernard What's that?
Gordon The eighth.
Joyce Fine.
Gordon Bernard?
Bernard Okay.
Margaret Dinner party. Sorry.
Gordon The ninth?
Margaret That's a Tuesday. Can't do Tuesdays.
Gordon The tenth?
Joyce Wednesday, Gordon. Shorthand.
Gordon The eleventh?
Joyce That's one of the alternate Thursdays I can't make. I'm all right for the
following Thursday.
Gordon That's the eighteenth.
Bernard No good.
Gordon You said you were all right for any other Thursday.
Bernard I didn't know the eighteenth was a Thursday, did I?
Gordon We're going to have to start looking at weekends.
Margaret Not weekends, Gordon. I'm sorry. Ryan would go spare. We have
all got other lives you know.
Gordon All right, all right! No weekends, no Tuesdays, no Wednesdays, no

alternate Thursdays. What about the following Monday...the twenty-second?

Joyce Yes.

Bernard Yes.

Margaret No.

Gordon Twenty-fifth.

Joyce Alternate Thursday.

Gordon Twenty-ninth?

Bernard I'm in Stockport.

Gordon The first.

Joyce It's my birthday.

Gordon Cancel it.

Joyce I can't!

Gordon Fine! Happy bloody birthday! Come to the rehearsal.

Joyce Trevor's taking me out.

Gordon We're all having to make sacrifices here, Joyce.

Joyce It's once a year, Gordon!

Gordon So's the panto. Put yourself out for once, Joyce.

Margaret Hang on, hang on. Crisis averted. What about the thirteenth? It's a Tuesday but I can make that one.

Gordon The thirteenth? Yes? (*General nodding*) Yes?? Everybody all right for the thirteenth? Hooray! (*He goes to write it in his diary*) Shit!

Margaret Problem, Gordon?

Gordon I can't make the thirteenth. Maureen's birthday. You understand, don't you, Joyce. All right, what about the twelfth?

Margaret Ah, now, that's the one Monday I *can't* make.

Gordon Fifteenth?

Bernard Is that a Thursday?

Gordon Yes, Bernard, that's a Thursday.

Bernard Er...no. Grimsby.

Gordon Nineteenth? (*There are various nods and shakings of heads which now eliminate all of the following dates*) Twenty-sixth. Twenty-ninth. Second. Ninth. Twelfth. Sixteenth. Twenty-third. Twenty-sixth. First. Seventh. (*There finally seems to be a consensus*) Yeah? Yes? We can all make the seventh? Excellent. Just as well really. That's the opening night. I suggest we start again - don't you?

Margaret Look, if it's any help, I'm all right for tomorrow night.

Joyce So am I.

Bernard Tomorrow's all right with me.

Gordon Marvellous. So tomorrow we'll have a quick read through at seven,

dress rehearsal at eight, and I'll see you all here again on opening night.
Margaret You don't think we're in danger of peaking too early, do you?
Gordon I'm going to the pub.

Gordon storms out.

Margaret He really can get so stroppy.

Lights to black. Music links to the next scene, where Gordon is handing out scripts to Joyce and Margaret. Bernard is not on stage.

Margaret I'm impressed, Gordon. It's actually typed up.
Gordon Not typed, Margaret. Little Grimley Amateur Dramatic Society has finally gone high-tech. This is laser-printed straight from my new word-processor.
Margaret Ooh!
Gordon (*handing Margaret another piece of paper*) What do you think, Margaret? My idea for the poster.
Margaret Oh, my God!
Joyce What is it?
Margaret No, I don't think you should see this, Joyce.
Joyce Oh, come on.
Gordon What's the problem, Margaret?
Margaret The title, Gordon. Really!
Gordon Marketing, Margaret. All designed to drag 'em in. Anybody seen Bernard?
Joyce Come on, show me!
Margaret No, Joyce. I mean, you're a member of the W.I.
Joyce If I'm going to be in it, Margaret, sooner or later I'll find out what it's called.
Gordon She has a point, Margaret. (*Shouting into the wings*) Bernard!
Margaret You've heard of Puss in Boots, Joyce.
Joyce Yes.
Margaret Well, add a Y.
Joyce (*after a long, thoughtful pause*) Puss in Bootys?
Margaret No, Joyce.
Gordon (*he opens the door flat again and peers in*) Bernard?
Bernard (*shouting from the lighting box*) I'm up here!
Gordon Come on down. We're starting.

Joyce I quite like Puss in Boots.

Gordon Well it's not exactly Puss in Boots, Joyce. I just used that as a snappy title. It's really Dick Whittington and his cat. I needed something with just two main female roles. Margaret's playing Dick.

Joyce And what am I playing, Gordon?

Gordon Have a guess, Joyce.

Joyce The cat, Gordon?

Gordon Astonishing. It's pure instinct with you, isn't it, Joyce.

Bernard enters. Throughout the scene he chain-eats bananas.

Bernard That lighting desk is a disaster waiting to happen.

Gordon Never mind that. Here.

Bernard You said I wasn't in it.

Gordon Look, it's just a small walk-on part, that's all. I promise.

Bernard Does it involve acting?

Gordon Don't be ridiculous.

Bernard All right. Ooh! New word processor?

Gordon Certainly is, Bernard.

Bernard Anyway, listen. If we don't get something done about that lighting desk we're going to have a serious problem.

Gordon Right, have a crack at it from the top.

Bernard He's not listening to me.

Gordon I'm listening Bernard, but I've got more important things to worry about at the moment, thank you.

Bernard I reckon the dimmers are sending too much power to the lamps.

Gordon Margaret, Joyce - you're both on. So, curtain, lights, overture, and...let's go! (*There's a bemused silence as they both look at the scripts*) Problem? You can read, can you?

Margaret We can read, Gordon. But we don't understand.

Gordon (*already getting tense and patronising*) Well, I'll try and help you, Margaret. Tell me, which word are you stuck on?

Margaret Well, Cas, for example.

Gordon Cas?

Margaret Yes, Cas, there look.

Gordon (*he struts over to check Margaret's script*) It's cat, Margaret. I'm terribly sorry if the odd typo has slipped through, I did do it in a rush. But I'm sure if you read it in context it's not so terribly difficult. Cat, Margaret. Dick Whittington and his Cat.

A Flying Ducks Publication

Joyce Whissingson.

Gordon What?

Joyce It says here, Dick Whissingson and hit Cas.

Margaret It's not the odd typo, Gordon. The whole thing's riddled with mistakes.

Bernard This new word processor of yours. You didn't get it from Brian Maynard, did you?

Gordon Might have done. Why? (*Bernard bursts into laughter*) Something amusing you, Bernard?

Bernard He tried that one on me.

Gordon He tried what one on you?

Bernard Dodgy software, mate. He got stuck with a job-lot. It's all right till you try and print it out - then all the T's come out as S's.

Joyce And what do the S's come out as?

Margaret T's by the look of it.

Gordon Wait till I get hold of him. All right, all right, we'll just have to battle through. I'm sure it won't be too bad if you keep your wits about you. I'll sort it out for next week. Come on, let's take it from the top of page one. Margaret's entrance.

Margaret "Here we are, old friend, London Sown."

Gordon Town.

Margaret "I muts tay, shit it..."

Gordon This is, Margaret.

Margaret It says "shit it", Gordon.

Gordon Just use your brain, Margaret. S's are T's, T's are S's. "This is..."

Margaret "This is...noshing like I wat expecsing".

Gordon Is that the best you can do, Margaret?

Margaret My fault, Gordon, I was expecting it to be in English.

Gordon All right, Joyce, you're on.

Joyce Right. Where from?

Gordon From where we just left off, Joyce.

Joyce Sorry, I must have missed it.

Gordon From the beginning of your first line.

Joyce Right.

Gordon And don't panic, Joyce. It's just one word, and it's got no S's or T's in it, so you should be off to a flying start.

Joyce Okay, here goes, then. (*Pause*) Ready?

Gordon Yes, Joyce, we're all here.

Joyce (*woodenly, after a preparatory cough*) Miaow.

A Flying Ducks Publication

Gordon Hold it, hold it. Cat, Joyce.

Joyce What?

Gordon Cat, Joyce. Cat.

Joyce What are you talking about, Gordon?

Gordon You're a cat, Joyce.

Joyce I know I'm a cat, Gordon.

Gordon Then do what cats do, Joyce.

Joyce I said miaow, Gordon, what more do you want me to do?

Gordon (*getting very wound up*) I want you to feel like a cat, Joyce! I want you to look like a cat!

Joyce Well I'm terribly sorry, Gordon! I'm sorry I haven't got four legs. I'm sorry I wasn't born with fur and whiskers.

Bernard Oh, I don't know - you've got the whiskers.

Gordon Think about the role, Joyce. Think what you are! It's not just what you say, but the way you move, the way you react. Become the part, Joyce. Adopt the essential feline characteristics.

Joyce I'm sorry?

Gordon Act like a frigging cat, Joyce.

Margaret Gordon! There's no need for that!

Gordon Well I'm sorry, Margaret, but it's no good her just standing there like a stuffed librarian and saying miaow, now is it!

Joyce Are you getting angry with me, Gordon?

Gordon (*ranting*) No I am not getting angry with you, Joyce! You wouldn't like me if I got angry with you.

Joyce Because you promised you wouldn't, Gordon, we had a deal.

Margaret (*aside*) Think of the accounts, Gordon.

Gordon (*with trembling self-restraint*) That was...excellent, Joyce. A good base on which to build. Perhaps, as we progress, you'd like to think about some of the finer details of the character.

Margaret Here's a little something I do, Joyce. Ask yourself this, "How would Meryl Streep say miaow?" It works for me.

Gordon Let's just...move on, shall we. Bottom of the page. Bernard, we're on.

Bernard Where?

Gordon Pantomime horse.

Bernard Which end am I?

Gordon The non-speaking end.

Bernard Suits me.

Gordon But I want you to do the sound effects of the hooves - there. Right?

Bernard Right.

A Flying Ducks Publication

Bernard crouches behind Gordon to form the horse, having just peeled another banana.

Gordon And watch what you're doing with that banana. Here we go.

Bernard bites into the banana, then starts saying "Clip-clop" with his mouth full.

Bernard Hip-hok..Slip-shok..

Gordon Bernard...Bernard. Let me give you a little acting tip. One of the finest thespians I ever had the pleasure to witness in live theatre was Sir John Gielgud. Now there, Bernard, was the consummate master of the English language. For sheer clarity of expression he was unsurpassed. His diction was impeccable. And guess what, Bernard? And I noticed this particularly. He hadn't got a banana in his mouth. Do you think there could be a connection?

Bernard This is my bloody tea. I don't have time to go home, you know, not like these part-time teachers.

Margaret I beg your pardon!

Gordon All right, all right. Let's compromise, can we, Bernard? What about if you only eat a banana between sentences. Okay. Let's try it again.

Bernard (*woodenly*) Clip-clop. Clip-clop. Clip-clop. Clip-clop.

Margaret One more.

Bernard What?

Margaret You've missed one.

Gordon It doesn't matter, Margaret.

Margaret Fine. If you're happy with sloppy performances, Gordon. I know if I were directing I'd come down on that sort of thing like a ton of bricks.

Bernard Clip-bloody-clop.

Margaret Thank you.

Gordon Happy now, Margaret?

Margaret If you can't be true to the essential text on the first read-though, Gordon, when can you?

Gordon Well, now it's your turn to be true to the essential text, Margaret.

Margaret What?

Gordon Read the words.

Margaret Oh, erm..."Woah, Neddy. Where are you going in tuch a hurry? My, my. You're a fine-looking animal.

Gordon "Thank you, kind sir".

Margaret This is a talking horse?

Gordon This is a talking horse, Margaret, yes. Do you have a problem with

that?

Margaret Well, let's face it, it is a little fantastic, isn't it, Gordon - but, oh well, as it's a panto.

Gordon Thank you, Margaret.

Bernard Hurry up, my bloody back's killing me.

Margaret Does it talk at both ends?

Gordon Just get on with it.

Margaret "Would you like so t...s...roke...stroke...to stroke!" I'm getting the hang of this now. "Would you like to stroke my putty". Oh, Gordon, I can't say that!

Gordon Trust me, Margaret. It'll go straight over the kids' heads.

Joyce I don't get it.

Gordon Don't worry about it, Joyce.

Joyce Why would a horse want to stroke a cat?

Margaret She has a point, Gordon. The whole scenario is seriously flawed. It simply isn't grounded in reality.

Just then, the middle area of the stage goes black, accompanied by a crackling noise.

Gordon What's going on?

Bernard I've been trying to tell you for the last hour. The dimmer rack's knackered. It's blowing the bulbs.

Joyce Well, as Treasurer, I would like to point out that we certainly cannot afford to replace them.

Gordon Why the hell are the stage lights on for a rehearsal anyway? What's wrong with the working lights?

Bernard They're not working.

Gordon This is ridiculous. How many lamps have we got left?

Bernard (*squinting into the lights*) Three. (*There's another crackle, and another area of stage goes black, leaving just two lit areas on the extreme sides*) Two.

They all huddle into one spotlit corner of the stage, looking dolefully up at the lights.

Gordon How much to replace the bulbs, Bernard?

Bernard What, that lot? About three hundred quid.

Gordon What?

Bernard That's if you can get the spares. Some of these lamps are so old they probably work on gas.

Joyce Well, as Treasurer, I would like to point out that we can't afford three

hundred pounds, Gordon.

Gordon All right, all right. Let's not panic. Joyce, how much have we got in the kitty?

Joyce Well, as Treasurer, perhaps this would be a good time to remind you that your membership subscriptions are now due. Five pounds each, please.

They all groan.

Gordon Come on, let's cough up.

Joyce Thank you, Gordon. Thank you, Margaret. Thank you, Bernard. Mine's already in.

Gordon So, how much have we got?

Joyce Twenty-two pounds.

Gordon Terrific. How much is one bulb, Bernard?

Bernard About thirty quid.

Gordon Good. Good-oh.

Bernard Course, unless we fix the dimmer rack, it could be a waste of money. You could put new lamps in and they still might blow. (*There's a crackle, and their spotlight goes out*) Like that.

They all crab across into the opposite spotlit area.

Gordon How much for a new dimmer rack?

Bernard About two grand.

Joyce Well, as Treasurer...

Gordon Shut up, Joyce! Let me think. Now, five performances, three pounds a ticket, times by...(*he mumbles some figures to himself, and then sighs thoughtfully*)

Margaret Well?

Gordon Well, I reckon if we don't do the panto, we might break even.

Margaret And if we do do the panto?

Gordon Don't even think about it, Margaret.

Margaret So it's all off, then.

Gordon Not quite. While there's light, there's hope. Bernard, I want you to re-focus that lamp.

Bernard Where to?

Gordon Everywhere, just fill the stage with it.

Bernard Don't hold your breath.

A Flying Ducks Publication

Bernard exits.

Gordon Margaret. There's obviously going to be no money for costumes, is there any chance...

Margaret My students are very busy, Gordon. It's coming up to their exams.

Gordon Please, Margaret. You know I only say please when I really, really want something.

Margaret Oh, I'll try and slip it through as a special end of term project.

Gordon Brilliant!

Margaret Though how I'll manage to pass off a pantomime horse as an exercise in haute couture God only knows. I'm sure they saw right through me last year.

Joyce We didn't get you into trouble, did we, Margaret?

Margaret Let's put it this way, Joyce. One minute I'm putting up Snow White posters in the canteen. The next minute I'm asking my students to start work on an ankle-length velvet dress with paper-doily sleeves, and seven matching outfits with pointed caps specially tailored for the shorter man. You don't exactly have to be Einstein to work it out, do you?

Bernard Just do the horse's body. I'll knock up the head.

Margaret Suits me. What else do you need?

Gordon Not much. An old dame for me - usual thing. Outrageous dress, monstrous breasts, stupid hat...

Margaret Joyce, could you ask your mother again?

Joyce I'll try.

Gordon Dick Whittington for you, of course, Margaret - tights, hankie on stick, cap, feather - oh, and a cat costume for Joyce - whiskers, ears, tail...(*he sighs*)...and the word CAT in really big letters across the back.

The spotlight cross-fades to a weak general light centre-stage.

Bernard (*shouting from the lighting box*) That's the best I can do.

Gordon Well, it's not exactly Pink Floyd in concert, but it'll have to do. Right, let's get on with the rehearsal. And let's all just pray, that it doesn't blow.

There a final "ping" and the stage is completely black. A cigarette lighter illuminates Gordon scrabbling in his pocket. He pulls out a cheque book.

Gordon Bernard. Go and buy us two hundred pounds worth of bulbs.

Joyce Gordon! Where are you going to get that sort of money?

A Flying Ducks Publication

Gordon I'm expecting a refund on a word processor.

Rousing pantomime music takes us into the next scene. It's the opening night, and excitement and confusion reign. Bernard is making a few last minute running repairs. He starts by hastily touching up a badly-made bench with white paint. Then he dashes off and returns with an equally badly-made sign, pointing the way to "LONDON, 1 MILE". He tries desperately to make it stand up next to the bench, but it continually falls.

Bernard Come on, you bugger. Stand up. (*He wedges it under the bench to make it stand*) That'll do.

Gordon, wearing heavily rouged cheeks, wig and hat, comes dashing in carrying a large colourful dress. He immediately sits on the bench in order to slip into the dress.

Gordon There must be two hundred people out there.
Bernard (*now diverted by another last-minute job, painting the eyes on the head of an awful paper-mache pantomime horse head*) Two hundred and thirty eight. Don't sit on the bench by the way.
Gordon Why?
Bernard (*looking round and seeing Gordon*) Doesn't matter. Fixed it now. I still say we should have tried this horse costume at the dress rehearsal.
Gordon It'll be all right.
Bernard What if the head doesn't fit?
Gordon Look, you just worry about your end, okay?
Bernard And you promise you didn't have a curry last night?
Gordon Just come and zip me up.
Bernard I can't, I've got that stage flat to mend yet.

Bernard, having finished decorating the now cross-eyed horse, dashes off momentarily to grab a length of wood. Joyce enters, wearing a cat costume, complete with springy tail.

Joyce How do I look?
Gordon Like a librarian wearing a cat costume.
Bernard (*re-entering with the wood*) Give me a hand, Joyce.
Joyce There's loads of people!
Bernard Hurry up. Just put your weight on there. That's it.

Joyce is directed to sit on a small workbench, across which Bernard has put the piece of timber, ready for sawing.

Gordon Has anybody seen my breasts?
Bernard (*sawing the wood*) What do they look like?
Gordon Two pink cushions.
Bernard Oh, sorry mate. I thought they were rubbish. I chucked 'em on the skip.
Gordon You did what?
Bernard It's all right, they're only outside, I'll dig them out in a minute. Okay Joyce, that'll do.

Joyce gets up. In Bernard's hand is a sawn-off piece of wood and also, as he suddenly notices to his horror, Joyce's tail. He gulps, and quickly hides the tail behind his back before Joyce notices.

Gordon I can't believe you threw my breasts on the skip.
Bernard I'm going, I'm going. Keep your hat on.

Bernard exits hastily.

Gordon My hat! Where's my hat?
Joyce It's on your head, Gordon. You're more nervous than I am!
Gordon There's a lot at stake. Now, remember what I told you, Joyce. Bend your legs, slink about the stage, use your claws like this, and don't forget to waggle your...Joyce! Where is it??

We hear Bernard shouting off-stage, pantomime style:

Bernard Look behind you!!
Gordon Bernard!!!!

Bernard enters, with a cushion, Joyce's tail and a roll of heavy-duty adhesive tape. Joyce, meanwhile, tries to take a look at her ex-tail, but succeeds only in spinning herself around like a dizzy kitten.

Bernard I've found one of them.
Gordon You've sawn Joyce's tail off!
Bernard It was an accident. I'm working on it. (*He shows Gordon the tape*)

Gordon Forget it. There's no time. She'll have to be a manx.
Bernard (*presenting the cushion*) Here. Watch out for the potato peelings.
Gordon Find the other one, Bernard! And hurry up!
Bernard What's the panic?
Gordon Bernard, it's quarter past seven!
Bernard Yeah, but you're not the dame till the second half. It's the horse first.
Gordon Shit!

He tears off the dress, back to audience, revealing that all his dark clothes underneath now have white paint stripes, courtesy of the bench.   Bernard concentrates on taping Joyce's tail back on.

Joyce When's the zebra come into it?
Bernard Keep still, Joyce.
Gordon Horse costume. Where's the bloody horse costume!
Bernard Over there. There you go, Joyce. Good as new.
Gordon Ten minutes!
Bernard I'll have another look in the skip.

Bernard exits. Gordon thrashes about getting into the horse costume, managing only to get legs and arms all into the wrong holes.

Gordon Twenty-past seven! Come on, Margaret, where the hell are you?

Joyce lets out a huge gasp of horror.

Joyce Oh no!
Gordon What?
Joyce Stay calm, Gordon.
Gordon (*suspiciously*) Why?
Joyce Because if you don't, you're going to get very angry.
Gordon Why, Joyce?
Joyce Well, I've forgotten to tell you something, Gordon.
Gordon (*keeping his temper just under control*) Yes.
Joyce And it's like...a really, really important thing.
Gordon Carry on, Joyce.
Joyce Oh, you're going to kill me, Gordon.
Gordon No, I'm not going to kill you, Joyce. Not yet.
Joyce Oh you will, Gordon.

A Flying Ducks Publication

Gordon Possibly when I hear it, Joyce, but not until.

Joyce When you said, like, you know, about Margaret, it reminded me.

Gordon Reminded you of what, Joyce?

Joyce She rang me last night, Gordon.

Gordon And?

Joyce And...she can't come, Gordon.

Gordon She can't come.

Joyce No.

Gordon I'm taking this very calmly, Joyce, as you can see, because I have no doubt it's a very bizarre, albeit slightly pathetic little first night joke between you and Margaret, in order to wind me up.

Joyce Well, you know how, after the dress rehearsal on Wednesday, Gordon, how you said to Margaret, "Break a leg".

Gordon Yes.

Joyce She's broken a leg, Gordon.

Gordon She's broken a leg.

Joyce And an arm.

Gordon Here we are, Joyce, five minutes before curtain up - our leading lady is not coming because she's broken two rather vital limbs - and you forgot to tell me?

Joyce I was too excited, Gordon.

Gordon I'm still being very calm, Joyce. You're not going to make a fool of me, do you understand? I am not going to blow my top, and then have Margaret suddenly step out here and...oh my God. I've just realized. You look frightened, Joyce. Which can only mean one of two things. Either you really are frightened, or you're...acting. She's not coming is she, Joyce.

Joyce No, Gordon.

Gordon What happened?

Joyce She slipped on a banana skin.

Gordon (*finally exploding*) Nobody slips on a banana skin, Joyce! What is this? What's happening to me? Am I living in a cartoon?

Joyce She did, Gordon. Apparently, after the dress rehearsal, there was a banana skin on the steps outside, and she...

Gordon Who the hell would leave a ban.....Bernard!!!!!

Bernard enters, eating an almost-finished banana, and carrying the other cushion.

Bernard Got it! Bit smelly though.

A Flying Ducks Publication

Gordon snatches the cushion, and grabs Bernard by the scruff of the neck.

Gordon Get your tights on!
Bernard Do what?
Joyce What are you saying, Gordon?
Gordon There are two hundred people out there, Joyce. And thanks to the Apeman of Little Grimley, our leading lady has broken her leg. (*He grabs the banana skin from Bernard, and tosses it across the stage, angrily*)
Bernard Oh, dear.
Gordon Bernard, you're playing Dick!
Bernard On your bloody bike, pal!
Gordon We have no choice.
Bernard I don't know the words!
Gordon That's no excuse. Margaret didn't know the words.
Bernard I can't act!
Gordon Ditto.
Bernard But who's going to play the back-end of the horse?
Gordon We'll manage, Bernard.
Joyce You can't have a man playing Dick Whittington, Gordon, it's perverse.
Gordon The decision's made, Joyce. Bernard is playing the lead.
Bernard Oh no he isn't!
Gordon Oh yes he is!
Bernard Oh no he isn't!
Gordon Oh yes he is!!

Then, from off-stage, a booming voice:

Margaret Oh, no he isn't!!

Margaret enters dramatically, dressed in her Dick Whittington costume. She walks with the aide of a crutch. Her one arm is in a sling, and bulging under her tights is a huge bandaged leg.

Gordon Margaret!
Margaret Did you honestly think I would just lie down and let this...this... banana-eating baboon ruin all my good work? I couldn't do it to my public.
Bernard Margaret enters carrying a limp.
Margaret One more word from you and this walking stick enters your mouth, sideways.

A Flying Ducks Publication

Bernard Come on, Margaret, show us your crutch.

Margaret swings for Bernard with the crutch. Gordon intervenes, hearing music.

Gordon Shut it! Listen. That's the overture. We're on! Can you do it, Margaret?

Margaret I'm ready, Gordon. Let's give 'em hell!

Gordon Positions everybody. Quick, Bernard, get in!

Bernard tries frantically to get into what holes are left in the tangled horse costume.

Gordon The head, Joyce! Put the horse's head on!

Joyce puts the horse's head on herself.

Joyce Right!

Gordon Not on you, you fool, on me!

Joyce Oh, right. Now?

Gordon Yes, now, Joyce! Quickly! Are you in, Bernard?

Bernard I can't get my leg over.

Margaret I'm hardly surprised.

Joyce finally rams on the head. Bernard is still struggling desperately, and the horse runs amok, dragging Bernard behind.

Gordon What's going on?

Bernard My bloody leg's stuck.

Gordon I can't see.

Bernard Neither can I.

Margaret Watch where you're going. Arrgh!

They crash into Margaret, knocking her over and leaving her sprawling. Joyce runs around screaming, being chased by the horse.

Gordon Stop pushing, Bernard!

Bernard I'm not pushing. It's you!

Margaret My crutch. I need my crutch.

The tangled mess careers towards the bench, knocking the sign over. Chaos reigns.

A Flying Ducks Publication

Gordon Bernard, where the hell are you?
Bernard Where the bloody hell do you think I am?
Gordon You forgot to put the eye holes in, you prat.
Bernard I can't think of everything.
Margaret Watch out for that banana skin!

The horse slips and collapses or, even better if possible, falls off the front of the stage. The music swells to a climax as the lights fade and the on-stage panic reaches its climax.

Joyce Gordon! The houselights are going down!
Gordon Get up, Bernard!
Bernard I think I've broken my bloody leg.
Joyce Gordon!
Gordon Don't panic, Joyce.
Joyce The curtains are opening!
Margaret Will somebody please grab my crutch!

The lights come up full. There's a huge crackle and, with the exception of one tight spotlight go out. The spotlight catches Joyce, frozen like a rabbit staring into a car's headlights.

Gordon Do something, Joyce. Do something!

There's a moment's silent panic, before Joyce finally seizes the moment, throws out her arms flamboyantly, and lets rip with the same song with which she began the play. Music swells. Lights to black. Curtain.